Land of Liberty

Oregon

by Mike Graf

Consultant:
Robert Irvine, Ph.D.
Adjunct Faculty in History
Eastern Oregon University

Capstone press
Mankato, Minnesota

Capstone Press
151 Good Counsel Drive • P.O. Box 669 • Mankato, Minnesota 56002
http://www.capstone-press.com

Library of Congress Cataloging-in-Publication Data
Graf, Mike.
    Oregon / by Mike Graf.
    p. cm.— (Land of liberty)
    Contents: About Oregon—Land, climate, and wildlife—History of Oregon—
Government and politics—Economy and resources—People and culture.
    ISBN 0-7368-2193-7
    1. Oregon—Juvenile literature. [1. Oregon.] I. Title. II. Series.
F876.3.G73 2004
979.5—dc21   2003000803

Summary: An introduction to the geography, history, government, politics, economy,
resources, people, and culture of Oregon, including maps, charts, and a recipe.

Editorial Credits

Amanda Doering, editor; Jennifer Schonborn, series and book designer; Enoch Peterson,
    illustrator; Jo Miller, photo researcher; Eric Kudalis, product planning editor

Photo Credits

Cover images: Mount Hood in December, Tom & Pat Leeson; Oregon coastline,
PictureQuest/Image Ideas, Inc.

Bettmann/Corbis, 30; Capstone Press/Gary Sundermeyer, 54; Corbis, 26; David Jensen, 8,
13, 45; Folio, Inc./David R. Frazier, 34; Folio, Inc./Rob Crandall, 39; Gary Braasch, 17,
18, 32–33, 40, 52; GeoIMAGERY/Sid & Shirley Rucker, 56; Getty Images/Hulton Archive,
23; Gnass Photo Images/Jon Gnass, 12, 63; Jefferson County Historical Society/Museum,
29; Northwest Museum of Arts & Culture/ Eastern Washington State Historical Society,
Spokane, WA, 28; One Mile Up, Inc., 55 (both); Oregon State Capitol/painting by Barry
Faulkner, 1938, 20; Oregon Tourism Commission/Agriculture, 42–43; Oregon Tourism
Commission/Charlie Borland, 46; Oregon Tourism Commission/Roy Shigley, 50–51;
Oregon Trail Museum Association, 24, 58; PhotoDisc, Inc., 1, 4, 57; The Viesti Collection,
Inc./Walter Bibikow, 14–15; Tom & Pat Leeson, 22; U.S. Postal Service, 59

Artistic Effects
Corel, Earthstar, PhotoDisc, Inc.

1 2 3 4 5 6 08 07 06 05 04 03

Table of Contents

Wizard Island rises out of Crater Lake. The island got its name because it looks like a wizard's hat.

Chapter 1

About Oregon

More than 7,000 years ago, a huge volcano erupted in what is now southern Oregon. The cone of the volcano caved in, leaving a deep bowl called a caldera. Over time, rain and snow filled the caldera forming Crater Lake.

On the surface, Crater Lake appears to be calm. The brilliant blue water reflects the Cascade Mountains. But scientists wonder if the lake is as calm below the surface. In 1988, 1989, and 2001, they used submarines to explore the bottom of Crater Lake. Scientists discovered many things from these examinations. They found pockets of warm water bubbling from the lake bottom. Some scientists believe the volcano that lies under Crater Lake will erupt again someday.

At 1,950 feet (594 meters) deep, Crater Lake is the United States' deepest lake. It is the seventh deepest lake in the world.

Crater Lake became Oregon's only national park in 1902. In 2002, Oregon celebrated the park's 100-year anniversary by rededicating the park. Artists also displayed works inspired by Crater Lake.

The Beaver State

Oregon's nickname is the Beaver State. In the early 1800s, settlers came to Oregon to trap beavers and sell their fur. Beavers were almost wiped out during the state's long fur trading history.

Oregon is in the northwestern part of the United States. Washington borders Oregon to the north. The Pacific Ocean crashes along Oregon's western coast. California and Nevada lie south of Oregon. Idaho lies east of Oregon.

Oregon is rich in beauty and history. Tourists come to see Oregon's mountains, coastline, waterways, and forests. In the 1800s, many people found homes in Oregon. Settlers came from the eastern United States after a long journey on the Oregon Trail. Other settlers came from Japan, China, Mexico, and other countries.

Oregon Cities

Legend

- American Indian Reservation
- ⭐ Capital
- ● City
- River

Scale
miles
40 80 120 160
40 80 120 160
meters

WASHINGTON

Columbia River

Umatilla American Indian Reservation

Portland
Hillsboro ●
Beaverton ● ● Gresham

⭐ Salem

Warm Springs American Indian Reservation

Snake River

● Corvallis

N
W E
S

Springfield
● ● Bend
Eugene

OREGON

IDAHO

Medford ●

PACIFIC OCEAN

CALIFORNIA

NEVADA

The Pacific Ocean rushes to meet Oregon's rocky cliffs during high tide. Sandy beaches are exposed during low tide.

Chapter 2

Land, Climate, and Wildlife

Oregon's landscapes include mountains, deserts, fertile valleys, and rugged coastlines. The state is divided into five main regions. The Coastal Region and the Willamette Valley lie in western Oregon. The Cascade Mountains make up central Oregon. The Columbia Plateau and the Basin and Range Region are located in eastern Oregon.

Coastal Region

The Coastal Region stretches along Oregon's western border. In some areas, the coastline spreads into sandy beaches. In other areas, rocky cliffs rise above the Pacific Ocean.

Past the coast, mountains cover most of the region. Along the northwest, the Coast Range rises from the cliffs. The Coast Range shelters the Willamette Valley from the heavy rain the coast receives. The Klamath Mountains occupy the southwestern corner of Oregon. Trees cover both of these mountain ranges.

Willamette Valley

Mountains surround the fertile Willamette Valley. The valley lies east of the Coastal Region and west of the Cascade Mountains.

The Willamette River winds through the center of the valley. The river gives life to rich farmland. Many of Oregon's crops are grown in the Willamette Valley.

Because crops grew well in the valley, most early Europeans settled there. With large cities like Portland, Salem, and Eugene, the valley is still Oregon's most populated area.

Cascade Mountains

The Cascade Mountains lie east of the Willamette Valley. This range stretches from northern California to Canada. Oregon's Cascades have many volcanic peaks, deep forests, and rivers. Snowfields and glaciers cover mountain peaks year-round.

Oregon's Land Features

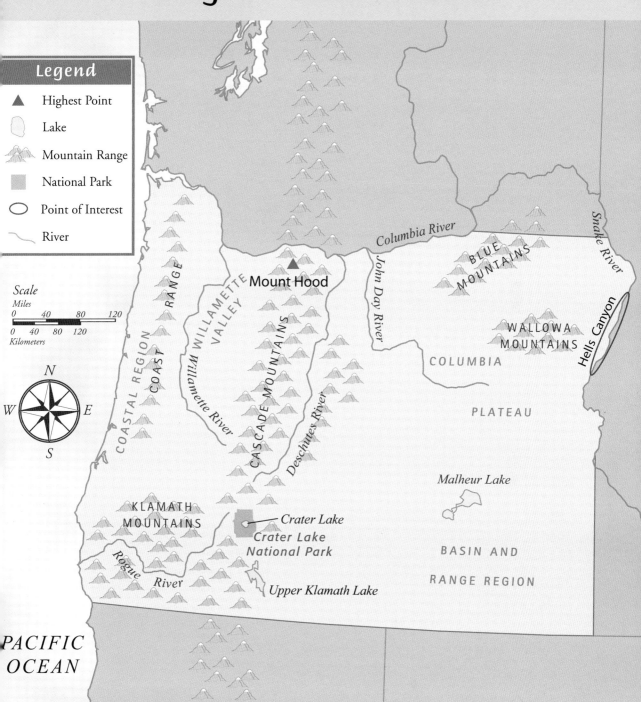

Legend

▲ Highest Point

Lake

Mountain Range

National Park

Point of Interest

River

Scale

Miles
0   40   80   120

0   40   80   120
Kilometers

N
W   E
S

COASTAL REGION

COAST RANGE

WILLAMETTE VALLEY

Willamette River

CASCADE MOUNTAINS

Mount Hood

Columbia River

John Day River

Deschutes River

BLUE MOUNTAINS

Snake River

WALLOWA MOUNTAINS

Hells Canyon

COLUMBIA

PLATEAU

Malheur Lake

KLAMATH MOUNTAINS

Crater Lake

Crater Lake National Park

Rogue River

Upper Klamath Lake

BASIN AND

RANGE REGION

PACIFIC OCEAN

Danger on Mount Hood

Mount Hood is the second most climbed mountain in the world. People have been climbing Mount Hood since the 1850s. In 1908, a guide service started leading climbers to the mountaintop. Since then, thousands of climbers have made it safely to the top. Some have not. About 130 people have died trying to climb Mount Hood since 1908.

Rescue teams are well trained and organized, but deaths still occur. In 1986, nine people froze to death while waiting out a storm. In 2002, groups of climbers fell into a deep crack in the snow. A rescue helicopter crashed while trying to carry out a climber. Three people were killed, and 12 were hurt.

Mount Hood is the tallest peak in Oregon. It rises to 11,239 feet (3,426 meters) above sea level. Mount Hood can easily be seen from Portland, which is 60 miles (97 kilometers) away.

Columbia Plateau

East of the Cascade Mountains lies the Columbia Plateau. This large region covers one-fourth of the state. The Columbia Plateau is less mountainous than western Oregon. But mountains do cover part of the region. The Blue Mountains and the Wallowa Mountains rise in northeastern Oregon.

Hells Canyon runs along the Oregon-Idaho border. Hells Canyon is the deepest canyon in the United States. At one point, the canyon is 8,032 feet (2,448 meters) deep.

The Snake River runs through the steep cliffs of Hells Canyon.

The Columbia Plateau is also good for agriculture. Farmers grow wheat, and ranchers raise livestock. Cattle and sheep graze on plateau grasslands.

Basin and Range Region

The Basin and Range Region lies southeast of the Cascade Mountains. This region is much flatter and drier than the rest of Oregon. The Basin and Range Region is called a high desert. It is the least populated region of Oregon.

Rivers and Lakes

The Columbia River is Oregon's largest river. It flows along the state's northern border between Oregon and Washington. The Columbia River begins in Canada and cuts west to the Pacific Ocean. Along the way, the river carves a passageway called the Columbia River Gorge. This area is known for its waterfalls and beautiful scenery. Multnomah Falls is a famous place in the Columbia River Gorge. At 620 feet (189 meters) high, it is the highest waterfall in the state.

Visitors can overlook the Columbia River Gorge from Crown Point State Scenic Corridor.

Oregon has other large rivers, including the John Day, the Deschutes, the Rogue, the Umpqua, and the Willamette Rivers. The Snake River runs along the Oregon-Idaho border.

Oregon also has 6,000 lakes. Malheur Lake is Oregon's largest natural lake. The lake is very shallow. It sometimes dries up into a muddy marsh.

Climate

Oregon's weather varies from the west to the east. Summers and winters are fairly mild in western Oregon. Temperatures in eastern Oregon are more extreme. On a winter night, temperatures may dip below 0 degrees Fahrenheit (minus 18 degrees Celsius). Summer temperatures are warm during the day, but nights are still cool.

Oregon's precipitation also varies from the west to the east. Western Oregon is cool, damp, and rainy. Eastern Oregon is much drier. The high peaks of the Cascade Mountains create a rain shadow. As storms come in from the Pacific Ocean, they drop their moisture on the western mountainsides. By the time the storm clouds move east, much of their moisture is gone. Snow and sleet can fall all across the state. The Cascade Mountains get the most snow.

Plant Life

The wet western side of Oregon is green with plants and trees. Deep forests and mossy areas with ferns cover the land. Western Oregon has forests of spruce, cedar, fir, and hemlock trees. Some of these trees are "National Championship Trees." This means they are the largest of their kind in the country.

Arms outstretched, several people try to circle one of Oregon's trees. Oregon is home to some of the largest trees in the country.

17

Eastern Oregon's plants are typical of a drier area. Shrubs are common. Ponderosa pines grow in some areas of eastern Oregon. In spring and summer, wildflowers cover the grasslands.

Wildlife

Oregon is home to many animals. Black bears are found mostly in the deep woods of southern Oregon. Mule deer, coyotes, and antelope are common in dry eastern Oregon. Mountain lions and bighorn sheep are found in mountainous areas.

The spotted owl has soft brown and white feathers. The owl's eyes are wide and dark, giving it a curious look.

Oregon's many rivers, lakes, and streams are home to several kinds of fish. Trout is often caught and eaten, but Oregon is famous for its salmon.

In 1999, salmon in the Columbia and Willamette Rivers were listed as endangered species. Some species of salmon are extinct. Many organizations are working to improve water conditions for salmon. Recently, salmon numbers have increased in some rivers.

Water birds live near Oregon's waters. Snow geese, cranes, gulls, and ducks stop at Malheur National Wildlife Refuge on Malheur Lake. They stop to rest and find food before moving on to summer or winter homes. Some birds raise their young at the refuge.

Spotted owls, an endangered species, live in Oregon's forests. They live in areas that have never been logged called old growth forests. Few of these areas remain in Oregon. Fewer than 4,000 owls make their homes in Oregon's trees. Logging has destroyed much of the owls' habitat. Logging is not allowed in certain areas so owls can live in their natural habitat.

Captain Robert Gray met friendly American Indians while sailing up the Columbia River.

Chapter 3

History of Oregon

American Indians were the first groups to settle in Oregon. Some tribes lived in Oregon for more than 10,000 years. Tribes living there included the Chinook, Umpqua, Klamath, Modoc, Shoshone, Nez Percé, and Yakama tribes.

European Explorers

European explorers came to North America looking for a passage connecting the Atlantic and Pacific Oceans through North America. The passage did not exist, but Oregon was explored in the process.

In 1792, American explorer Captain Robert Gray sailed up the Columbia River. He named the river after his ship.

Fort Clatsop

In December 1805, the Lewis and Clark party built Fort Clatsop near present-day Astoria. The party spent the winter at Fort Clatsop before heading back east. The fort was named for the friendly Clatsop Indians that lived in the area.

The fort was destroyed over time. Visitors can see a reconstruction of it at the Fort Clatsop National Memorial park.

Lewis and Clark

In the early 1800s, President Thomas Jefferson wanted to explore the land west of the Mississippi River. This land, bought from France, was called the Louisiana Purchase. The purchase doubled the size of the United States. Jefferson also wanted to find a water route to the Pacific Ocean. He sent Meriwether Lewis and William Clark to travel to the West Coast.

On November 7, 1805, Lewis, Clark, and a group of about 30 men reached the Pacific Ocean. They had been traveling for 18 months. The group built Fort Clatsop and stayed there for the winter before returning east. Lewis and Clark were the first known white Americans to cross the continent.

Along their journey, Lewis and Clark kept journals of the people and situations they encountered. They described the fertile lands in Oregon and the many furbearing animals. Farmers, fur trappers, and traders became excited about the opportunities the new land offered.

Sacagawea (right), a young Shoshone Indian woman, interpreted for Lewis and Clark. She knew many American Indian languages. Sacagawea traveled with Lewis and Clark and helped guide them safely through American Indian territories.

Wagon trails wound through the Barlow Cutoff of the Oregon Trail. Teams of oxen or mules pulled the wagons. People often walked to make the load lighter.

The United States and Great Britain both claimed Oregon. In 1818, the two countries agreed to share the land.

New Settlers and the Oregon Trail

In the 1820s, a few fur trappers and missionaries settled in the Willamette Valley. Dr. John McLoughlin founded Fort Vancouver on the Columbia River. McLoughlin helped many of the new settlers who came looking for land and furs. He was named the Father of Oregon.

From the 1840s to the 1860s, thousands of settlers poured into Oregon. They were seeking land. Many settlers came on a wagon route called the Oregon Trail. The Oregon Trail ran 2,200 miles (3,540 kilometers) from Independence, Missouri, to Oregon City. More than 300,000 people traveled west, but not everyone made it to Oregon.

The journey to Oregon was difficult. Many people died along the way from disease, hunger, and accidents. The last part of the journey was usually the hardest. Travelers had to cross Oregon's rivers and mountains to get to the Willamette Valley.

Many travelers were afraid of being attacked by American Indians. But few Indian attacks on travelers occurred. Most American Indians were friendly and traded with travelers.

Territory and Statehood

As more settlers came, people talked about making Oregon a state. At the time, Oregon covered a much larger area of land. In 1846, Great Britain gave up its claim to present-day Oregon and Washington. In 1848, the U.S. Congress named this area Oregon Territory. Colonel Joseph Lane became Oregon Territory's governor. Oregon City became the territory's capital.

The territory's population continued to grow in the 1850s. Many settlers from the east came in search of gold in California and Oregon. Settlers also came to farm the rich land.

In 1853, the Oregon Territory was divided. The northern part became Washington Territory. On February 14, 1859, the southern part became the state of Oregon. The capital was moved from Oregon City to Salem.

Colonel Joseph Lane became the first governor of Oregon Territory. He also served as an Oregon representative in the U.S. Congress.

"You might as well expect the rivers to run backward as that any man who was born free should be contented when penned up and denied liberty to go where he pleases."

—Chief Joseph, leader of the Nez Percé Indians

American Indian Conflicts

As more people moved into Oregon, conflicts between settlers and American Indians became more frequent. Oregon's new settlers were taking American Indian land. The new settlers also brought diseases that killed thousands of American Indians.

In 1851, settlers killed many American Indians who were trying to defend their land. The settlers wanted to establish a settlement at Port Orford. These killings led to more battles between settlers and American Indians. Settlers and American Indians signed many treaties, but settlers wanted the land. American Indians were forced onto reservations.

In 1877, the U.S. government tried to move the Nez Percé tribe off their lands in northeastern Oregon. The government wanted to move the tribe onto a reservation. The Nez Percé refused, but they knew they were no match for the U.S. Army. They tried to flee to Canada for safety. The army followed them and trapped them in Montana. The Nez Percé leader, Chief Joseph, surrendered. His tribe was hungry. Some were freezing to death. The U.S. government sent the Nez Percé to a reservation in Indian Territory, which was present-day Oklahoma. There, many of the people died of disease and hunger. In 1885, the tribe relocated to Washington.

Growth and Industry

Logging started in Oregon in the late 1800s. Oregon quickly became one of the largest timber-producing states in the country.

Chief Joseph led his people through Idaho, Wyoming, and Montana to avoid war with the U.S. military. Chief Joseph died in 1904 without ever returning to Oregon.

Railroad workers built the Oregon Trunk Railroad by laying down logs for the base of the railroad. Metal tracks and ties were put over the logs.

Workers built railroads in the late 1800s and early 1900s. Railroads made it much easier to transport goods to the east. They also brought more settlers to live and work in the state.

Thousands of immigrants came to Oregon in the late 1800s and early 1900s. Many of these immigrants came from China, Japan, and the Philippines. They worked building railroads and

Portland shipbuilders lay the bottom of a ship, called the keel. This ship was built in just 10 days in 1942.

in canning factories for very low pay. Many of these immigrants were treated poorly by whites.

The Great Depression and World War II

The Great Depression (1929–1939) hit the United States and Oregon hard. Many Oregonians lost their jobs and land.

President Roosevelt set up the Civilian Conservation Corps (CCC) to provide jobs and preserve nature. In Oregon, the CCC worked building trails, dams, bridges, and roads.

World War II (1939–1945) helped end the Great Depression. The war brought many new jobs to Oregon. Workers built ships on the coast. Several military camps trained soldiers.

After the Japanese bombed Pearl Harbor, Hawaii, in 1941, Japanese Americans in Oregon were treated unfairly. The U.S. government moved Japanese Americans in California, Oregon, and Washington to camps. This practice was called relocation. Many Japanese Americans lost their homes, land, and possessions because of relocation.

The only two enemy attacks on the mainland United States during World War II happened in Oregon. In 1942, a Japanese submarine fired at Fort Stevenson at the mouth of the Columbia River. In 1945, a family was killed by a Japanese bomb attached to a balloon.

Late 1900s and Beyond

In the 1960s and 1970s, Oregon began dealing with the problems of growing industry and a growing population. Pollution was one of the biggest problems. Farm chemicals and waste threatened the Willamette River. The state government passed many laws to control pollution of Oregon's waterways.

More recently, Oregon has experienced other environmental setbacks. In February 1996, between 19 and 30 inches (48 and 76 centimeters) of rain fell in less than four days. The Great Flood of 1996 caused millions of dollars in damage in the Willamette Valley.

In summer 2002, one of the largest forest fires in Oregon's history swept through southern Oregon. Lightning strikes started two fires, which became one huge blaze. Thousands of acres of land and forests burned.

A man wades through the streets of a town flooded by the Nehalem River. The 1996 flood caused millions of dollars in damage to homes and businesses.

Oregon's capitol looks very modern.
It was built in 1938 after the
previous capitol burned down.

Chapter 4

Government and Politics

The people of Oregon Territory were eager to become a state. The state constitution was written and approved almost two years before Oregon was allowed into the Union. In February of 1859, Oregon Territory became the 33rd state, and the constitution went into effect.

Branches of Government

Oregon's constitution divides the state government into three branches. They are the executive, the legislative, and the judicial branches.

Oregon's executive branch carries out laws. The governor heads the executive branch. The governor signs or rejects

Did you know...?
Since 1951, self-service gas stations have been illegal in Oregon. Oil companies and gas station owners have not been able to have the law changed. New laws allow motorcyclists to pump their own gas. Vehicle drivers must still have their gas pumped by gas station attendants.

suggested laws. He or she also plans a budget for the state and appoints officials to state departments. The other five officials in the executive branch answer directly to the governor. All six officials serve four-year terms.

The legislative branch makes laws. This branch also helps plan budgets and discusses issues that affect Oregon. The legislature can pass laws that have been rejected by the governor if enough members agree. The senate and the house of representatives make up the legislative branch. Oregon's 30 senators are elected to four-year terms. Sixty representatives make up the house of representatives. Each representative is elected to a two-year term.

Oregon's judicial branch interprets laws and tries court cases. The lowest state courts are circuit and tax courts. Circuit courts hear criminal and juvenile cases. Tax courts hear tax law cases. If the outcome from a lower court case is challenged, the case is retried in the court of appeals. Oregon's

Oregon's State Government

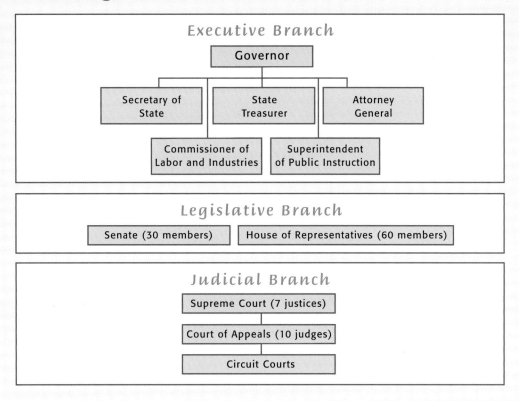

Executive Branch

Governor

Secretary of State | State Treasurer | Attorney General

Commissioner of Labor and Industries | Superintendent of Public Instruction

Legislative Branch

Senate (30 members) | House of Representatives (60 members)

Judicial Branch

Supreme Court (7 justices)

Court of Appeals (10 judges)

Circuit Courts

supreme court is the highest court in the state. It has seven justices. All Oregon judges are elected to six-year terms.

National Government and Politics

Oregon also takes part in the national government. Like all U.S. states, Oregon sends two senators to the U.S. Senate. Oregon also sends five representatives to the U.S. House of Representatives.

"The most important issue facing Oregon's forests today is how to manage them."

—Arlene M. Whalen, Public Information Officer,
Oregon Department of Forestry

Oregon's voters usually do not favor one political party more than another. In the 1990s and early 2000s, Oregonians have voted Democratic in presidential elections. In state politics, Oregonians support candidates of both the Republican and Democratic parties. Rural areas of the state typically support Republican candidates. Large cities tend to support Democratic candidates. The state also has a large number of Independent Party voters.

Environmental Laws

Oregonians want to protect their forests, rivers, and natural resources. Oregon's lawmakers try to balance the needs of industry with the needs of the environment.

Oregon made environmental laws and departments before most states did. In 1911, Oregon created a Department of Forestry. The department's job was to reduce forest fires on private lands. In 1929, the state passed a law to replace trees in logged areas.

Mark Hatfield

Oregonian Mark Hatfield never lost an election in his career. In 1956, he was elected Oregon's secretary of state. At age 34, he was the youngest person in Oregon history to hold that office. He was elected governor in 1958 and reelected in 1962. This election made him the first two-term governor of Oregon in the 1900s. In 1966, he was elected to the U.S. Senate. He served in the Senate for over 30 years. Hatfield retired in 1997.

In the 1960s and 1970s, many laws were passed to protect the environment. Laws passed in 1967 controlled how much waste could be dumped into the Willamette River. In 1970, the Scenic Waterways Act was passed to protect Oregon's rivers. A 1971 law banned bottles that could not be recycled or turned in for deposit. Another law required logging companies to protect the water, plants, and animals of the forests while logging. In 1975, Oregon became the first state to ban aerosol cans. Aerosol cans used to contain chemicals that hurt the environment.

Forestry workers cut a
log into pieces to make
it easier to transport.

Chapter 5

Economy and Resources

Oregon's early economy depended on agriculture, fishing, and forestry. These industries are still important to the success of the state. More recently, manufacturing and tourism have become large industries.

Forestry and Agriculture

One of Oregon's largest industries is forestry. Almost half of the state is forested. Oregon wood becomes logs, boards, cardboard, and paper products. Recently, timber harvests have decreased. Some of the decrease is due to laws that preserve and protect forests. Oregon requires land owners to reforest, or replant trees, after a timber harvest. Reforestation is good for the environment. It also assures that the forest industry will have a future in Oregon.

Agriculture accounts for one-fifth of Oregon's economy. Oregon is the nation's top producer of Christmas trees, hazelnuts, grass seed, peppermint, black raspberries, and blackberries. Oregon's Willamette Valley also grows many other kinds of fruits and vegetables. Farmers grow wheat in the Columbia Plateau.

Livestock and dairy products also are a part of Oregon's agriculture. Ranchers herd sheep and cattle in the Columbia Plateau. Dairy farms in western Oregon produce milk and cheese.

Manufacturing

Manufacturing is another large part of Oregon's economy. Products made in the state include electronics, metal products, food products, and forest products.

Making high-technology products has recently become a large part of Oregon's manufacturing industry. Almost one-third of Oregon's manufacturing workers are employed by high-technology companies. Computer companies like Hewlett-Packard and Intel have factories in Oregon's Willamette Valley.

Wheat fields blanket many parts of the Columbia Plateau. Wheat is used to make bread, cereal, and other food products.

Tourism

Tourism has become a big business in
Oregon. Vacationers spend more than
$6 billion per year in the state. Many
people come to enjoy the beautiful scenery
and year-round outdoor activities that Oregon
offers. Tourists ski, hike, bike, boat, mountain climb, fish, and
camp in Oregon's many wilderness areas. Tourism creates the
need for hotels, restaurants, and tour guides. These businesses
create jobs for Oregonians.

Natural Resources

Forests are Oregon's most important natural resource. The
state's forests create jobs in forestry, parks and recreation, and
tourism. Since logging has declined, the use of forests has
shifted to recreation. The state government has set aside parks
and reserves for people to enjoy nature.

Building materials, gold, and sources of energy also are
found in Oregon. Sand, gravel, and stone are mined to make
roads and buildings. Gold is still mined in parts of eastern
and central Oregon. The Mist Gas Field in northwestern

Tourists come to camp and hike in Oregon's beautiful Wallowa Mountains.

Oregon is the only natural gas field in the Pacific Northwest. Hydroelectric dams on the Columbia and Deschutes Rivers provide some of Oregon's energy needs.

Fishing also helps the state's economy. Sport and commercial fishing is very popular in Oregon. The state is famous for its river salmon. Many fisheries line Oregon's Pacific coast.

Visitors admire the sand sculptures created at the Cannon Beach Sand Castle Contest.

Chapter 6

People and Culture

Oregon is home to more than 3.4 million people. About three-fourths of these people live west of the Cascade Mountains. Portland, Salem, Eugene, and other cities grow as more people move there from rural areas.

Festivals

Oregonians celebrate many festivals outdoors. Cannon Beach hosts a sand sculpture contest every July. Participants have 12 hours to build their sculptures. People build castles, cars, animals, and other sand creations. A world-famous Shakespeare festival is held in Ashland. Many tourists come to see plays performed in outdoor theaters.

Oregonians love to celebrate nature and beauty. The Florence Rhododendron Festival celebrates the arrival of spring. Rhododendrons are plants with large, colorful flowers that bloom in May. The plants grow all over western Oregon. Two million people attend Portland's Rose Festival each year. Portland is called the "City of Roses." Visitors to the famous Rose Festival can see thousands of roses of different varieties. Parades, boat races, and music add to the celebration.

Many ethnic groups in the state celebrate their cultural backgrounds. The city of Portland celebrates the Hispanic holiday Cinco de Mayo on May 5. Also in Portland, Chinese American Oregonians celebrate the Chinese New Year. At the celebration, performers dance and people set off fireworks. The community of Mount Angel celebrates a German Oktoberfest. American Indians celebrate with powwows where they dance, tell stories, and make crafts. They also have an all-Indian rodeo in the Tygh Valley in northern Oregon.

Oregon's Ethnic Backgrounds

Most Oregonians have European backgrounds. Their ancestors come from England, Switzerland, Ireland, Scotland, Germany, Poland, and Italy. Some of these early settlers came from the eastern United States over the Oregon Trail.

Oregon's Ethnic Backgrounds

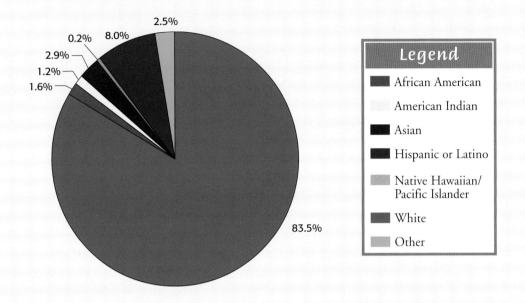

2.5%

0.2% 8.0%

2.9%

1.2%

1.6%

83.5%

Legend

■ African American

▨ American Indian

■ Asian

■ Hispanic or Latino

▨ Native Hawaiian/
Pacific Islander

■ White

■ Other

Hispanic Americans are Oregon's second largest ethnic group. Most Hispanic Americans in Oregon have Mexican backgrounds. They often work on farms and ranches. Large populations of Hispanic Americans also live in cities like Portland and Salem.

Chinese, Japanese, and Filipino immigrants came to the state in the late 1800s and early 1900s. They worked on the railroads and in canneries. Today, many Japanese Oregonians grow fruit in the Hood River Valley. This area is now known as Oregon's "Fruit Loop."

Many Asians have come to Oregon in recent years. Many of them run restaurants or small businesses. Portland and Beaverton are home to the state's largest populations of Asian Americans.

American Indians have lived in Oregon for thousands of years. Many American Indians in Oregon live on reservations. Some of the larger reservations are Warm Springs, Umatilla, Grand Ronde, and Siletz.

Sports

Basketball is the only sport in which Oregon has a professional team. The NBA Trailblazers are based in Portland. The state is also home to minor league hockey and baseball teams. Many people enjoy going to sporting events.

One of the world's largest rodeos is held in Pendleton. Rodeo participants compete in horse and steer roping, barrel jumping, and bull riding. People not only participate in rodeos, but also attend parades, dances, and shows.

Dust flies as cowboys try to rope wild horses at the Pendleton Round-Up. Every year in September, thousands of people gather in Pendleton to watch or participate in this four-day competition.

Oregonians of all ages ski at the Timberline ski area on Mount Hood.

Oregonians Outdoors

Oregonians take advantage of the nature around them. Oregon is home to 14 national forests and 35 wilderness areas. The state also has 13 downhill ski resorts. Some of the resorts offer skiing year-round. The Oregon coast attracts residents with beaches, tide pools, campgrounds, and seaside towns. Many bikers ride down the Oregon coast in summer. Oregon also is full of mountains with lakes and campgrounds. Oregonians hike, rock climb, cross-country ski, fish, and camp in the mountains. Oregonians also enjoy boating and kayaking in clear mountain lakes and rivers.

Preserving History

Oregonians preserve their history at the End of the Oregon Trail Interpretive Center in Oregon City. Visitors to the center learn about the lives of travelers on the Oregon Trail. The center is shaped like three covered wagons. The center offers exhibits, theater presentations, and crafts to educate visitors.

The High Desert Museum in Bend educates visitors about Oregon's high desert. Visitors can see live animals from the high desert region. They can also participate in historical exhibits and living history demonstrations.

Oregon has dealt with many changes throughout its history. One thing that remains the same is Oregonians' love for their beautiful state. The people of Oregon are determined to protect and preserve the land. They want their children and grandchildren to enjoy nature in its purest form.

Recipe: Berry Cobbler

Farmers in Oregon grow many kinds of berries. The state is the largest producer of raspberries and blackberries. Use these berries to make a delicious desert.

Ingredients

6 cups (1.5 liters) fresh or frozen raspberries, blueberries, blackberries, strawberries, or a combination of berries
1 cup (240 mL) flour
1 cup (240 mL) sugar
1½ teaspoons (7.5 mL) baking powder
½ teaspoon (2.5 mL) salt
¾ cup (175 mL) milk
½ cup (120 mL) butter
½ cup (120 mL) sugar
8 ounces (225 grams) whipped topping

Equipment

mixing bowl
dry-ingredient measuring cups
liquid measuring cup
measuring spoons
small microwave-safe bowl
9- by 13-inch (23- by 33-centimeter) baking dish
pot holders

What You Do

1. If using fresh berries, wash the berries, drain, and set aside.

2. Preheat the oven to 350°F (180°C).

3. Mix flour, 1 cup (240 mL) sugar, baking powder, salt, and milk in mixing bowl. Set aside.

4. Place butter in microwave-safe dish and heat on high for 30 seconds or until melted.

5. Pour melted butter into the baking dish.

6. Pour the flour and sugar mixture over the melted butter.

7. Place berries on top of the mixture.

8. Sprinkle ½ cup (120 mL) sugar on top of berries.

9. Bake for 45 minutes until cobbler is golden brown.

10. Serve with whipped topping.

Makes 8 servings

Oregon's Flag and Seal

Oregon's Flag

The Oregon state flag is blue with gold lettering and symbols. Blue and gold are the state's colors. The shield is surrounded by 33 stars. Above the shield are the words, "State of Oregon." Below the shield, the date of statehood, 1859, is written. On the reverse side of the flag is a beaver, the state animal. Oregon is the only U.S. state that has a different pattern on the back of the flag. The Oregon state flag was adopted in 1925.

Oregon's State Seal

Oregon's state seal has a shield bordered by 33 stars. The shield is divided by a ribbon that reads, "The Union." Above the ribbon are the mountains and forests of Oregon. A covered wagon and a team of oxen represent the settlers who came to Oregon. A British ship is shown leaving, while an American ship arrives. Below the shield is a sheaf of wheat, a plow, and a pickax, which all represent the state's agriculture. Above the shield is the American eagle.

Almanac

General Facts

Nickname: Beaver State

Population: 3,421,399 (U.S. Census 2000)
Population rank: 28th

Capital: Salem

Largest cities: Portland, Salem, Eugene, Gresham, Beaverton

Agriculture

Agricultural products: Timber, hazelnuts, berries, greenhouse and nursery products, wheat, cattle

Climate

Average winter temperature: 34 degrees Fahrenheit (1 degree Celsius)

Average summer temperature: 64 degrees Fahrenheit (18 degrees Celsius)

Average annual precipitation: 26.5 inches (67 centimeters)

Geography

Area: 98,386 square miles (254,820 square kilometers)
Size rank: 9th

Highest point: Mount Hood, 11,239 feet (3,426 meters) above sea level

Lowest point: Pacific Coast, sea level

Western meadowlark

Beaver

Symbols

Animal: Beaver

Bird: Western meadowlark

Fish: Chinook salmon

Flower: Oregon grape

Insect: Swallowtail butterfly

Economy

Natural resources: Timber, fish, sand, gravel

Types of industry: Forest products, agriculture, tourism, manufacturing, technology

Symbols

Motto: "She flies with her own wings"

Nut: Hazelnut

Song: "Oregon, My Oregon," written by J. A. Buchanan, composed by Henry Murtagh

Tree: Douglas fir

Government

First governor: John Whiteaker, 1859–1862

Statehood: February 14, 1859, 33rd state

U.S. Representatives: 5

U.S. Senators: 2

U.S. electoral votes: 7

Counties: 36

Timeline

State History

1500s

About 100 American Indian tribes live in Oregon.

1805

Lewis and Clark reach the Pacific Ocean at the mouth of the Columbia River.

1877

U.S. troops battle the Nez Percé Indians; the Nez Percé surrender in Montana.

1792

Captain Robert Gray sails into the Columbia River and names the river after his ship.

1840–1860

More than 300,000 settlers travel the Oregon Trail; Oregon becomes a territory in 1848 and a state in 1859.

U.S. History

1775–1783

Colonists fight for independence from the British in the Revolutionary War.

1861–1865

The Union and the Confederacy fight the Civil War.

1620

Pilgrims settle in North America.

58

Greetings from OREGON
USA 34
2002

1942
A Japanese submarine fires at Fort Stevenson in one of the only attacks on the U.S. mainland in World War II.

1960s and 1970s
Oregon's government passes many laws to reduce pollution and clean up the environment.

2002
Fires sweep through southern Oregon, destroying thousands of acres of forests.

1902
Crater Lake National Park becomes Oregon's only National Park.

1929–1939
The United States faces economic hardship in the Great Depression.

1964
Congress passes the Civil Rights Act, making discrimination illegal.

1914–1918
World War I is fought; the United States enters the war in 1917.

1939–1945
World War II is fought; the United States enters the war in 1941.

2001
Terrorists attack the World Trade Center and the Pentagon on September 11.

Words to Know

caldera (kal-DER-ah)—a collapsed volcano; Crater Lake is a caldera filled with water.

Civilian Conservation Corps (CCC)—an agency that was created during and after the Great Depression to preserve nature and create jobs; the CCC worked to build roads, bridges, and trails in Oregon.

dormant (DOR-muhnt)—not active; Mount Hood is a dormant volcano.

gorge (GORJ)—a deep valley with steep, rocky sides

precipitation (pri-sip-i-TAY-shuhn)—the falling of water from the sky in the form of rain, snow, sleet, or hail

rain shadow (RAYN SHAD-oh)—a region that receives less rain because of high mountains

reforestation (re-FOR-ist-AY-shuhn)—the replanting of trees after cutting them down

relocation (re-loh-KAY-shuhn)—the practice of moving people; Japanese Americans in Oregon were relocated to camps during World War II.

To Learn More

Ingram, Scott. *Oregon, the Beaver State.* World Almanac Library of the States. Milwaukee: World Almanac Library, 2002.

Jaffe, Elizabeth D. *The Oregon Trail.* Let Freedom Ring. Mankato, Minn.: Bridgestone Books, 2002.

Lassieur, Allison. *The Nez Percé Tribe.* Native Peoples. Mankato, Minn.: Bridgestone Books, 2000.

Shannon, Terry Miller. *Oregon.* From Sea to Shining Sea. New York: Children's Press, 2003.

Internet Sites

Do you want to find out more about Oregon?
Let FactHound, our fact-finding hound dog, do the research for you.

Here's how:
1) Visit *http://www.facthound.com*
2) Type in the Book ID number:
   0736821937
3) Click on FETCH IT.

FactHound will fetch Internet sites picked by our editors just for you!

Places to Write and Visit

Oregon Department of Fish and Wildlife
P.O. Box 59
2501 Southwest First Avenue
Portland, OR 97207

Oregon Historical Society
1200 Southwest Park Avenue
Portland, OR 97203-2483

Oregon Recreation Guide
Salem District
1717 Fabry Road Southeast
Salem, OR 97306

Oregon Secretary of State
136 State Capitol
Salem, OR 97310-0722

Mount Hood's snowcapped peak can be seen in the distance from Portland's skyline.

Index